SECRETS OF
SMITH WIGGLESWORTH

Personal Insights Into the
Miracle Life of God's General

by W. Hacking

D0963794

HARRISON HOUSE
Tulsa, Oklahoma

Unless otherwise indicated, all Scripture quotations are taken from the *King James Version* of the Bible.

Secrets of Smith Wigglesworth—
Personal Insights Into the Miracle Life of God's General
ISBN 1-57794-514-X
Copyright © 2002 by W. Hacking

Formerly entitled, *Smith Wigglesworth—*
A Life Ablaze With the Power of God
ISBN 0-89274-785-4
Copyright © 1995 by Harrison House, Inc.

Formerly entitled, *Smith Wigglesworth Remembered*
Copyright © 1981 by Harrison House, Inc.

Formerly entitled, *Reminiscences of Smith Wigglesworth*
ISBN 0-904229-00-9
Copyright © 1972 by W. Hacking

06 05 04 03   10 9 8 7 6 5 4 3

Published by Harrison House, Inc.
P.O. Box 35035
Tulsa, Oklahoma 74153

Dedication

I dedicate this little book to my dear wife
who for nearly fifty years has been my life partner
in Pentecostal service and ministry.

Contents

Preface

This little book is exactly what it claims to be. It is not a biography, for I am not the one to write the biography of Smith Wigglesworth. I write only from my own contact with him.

There are others who could write more, but as yet they have not done so. After long consideration, I wrote under compulsion, feeling that something more should be made public about this God-anointed servant of God who during his ministry brought great blessing, inspiration, and deliverance to so many.

I have received such blessing in writing this book (and especially in recording the notes from his messages).

I feel sure that my readers will receive fresh inspiration for vital Christian living and a great challenge to daring faith.

—W. Hacking

Foreword

Smith Wigglesworth was a household name in Pentecostal circles for more than a generation. Today, he is still one of the most referred-to names in Pentecostal preaching and writing.

Often called *the apostle of faith,* he boldly preached divine healing and the Full Gospel message all over the world, when few others (apart from the Bosworth brothers and Maria Woodworth-Etter) were known in this field.

Although he was not a writer, volumes of his messages still go through edition after edition, while his biography continues to be on nearly every Pentecostal preacher's bookshelf.

This book by my dear friend and fellow laborer in the Gospel, William Hacking, will be particularly welcome. It is the first book written of personal reminiscences of Smith Wigglesworth.

Brother Hacking was in constant ministerial contact with him for a period of over twenty-five years. His book reveals much of the inner heart and character of this great man of God: his eminently human nature, his understanding of others, his compassion for the unsaved, the sick, and the needy.

Personally, I am deeply grateful for these refreshing memories. I have benefited much from reading them.

I knew Brother Wigglesworth first in 1918 when he visited our Assembly in Halifax. In 1919 I attended his famous Bradford Convention and in 1920 was a missionary candidate on the platform.

Smith Wigglesworth had a missionary heart. He gave his daughter as a missionary first to Angola, then to South America and later, as Mrs. James Salter, to the Congo Evangelistic Mission.

He gave me a valuable watch when I left for the Congo in 1924. In 1929 while on furlough, I sometimes drove him to various places to pray for the sick. I was much moved when he insisted on giving me half of any ministry gift he received on such occasions.

Regularly during his great campaigns in various parts of the world, he would accept only one evening offering towards his support, but insisted that a second one go to help the work in the Congo.

I can warmly recommend this intimate and revealing book and pray that the incidents recounted, along with the sayings of the last chapter, will stir many to believe God for greater things in their lives and ministry.

Harold Womersley
Former Field Superintendent
Evangelistic Mission
Congo (formerly Zaire)

1

On Fire for God

A life of fire. A life ablaze with God. This surely describes God's servant, Smith Wigglesworth. In one of his letters to me, dated November 21, 1940, he writes:

> Pleased to receive the news of much blessing on your ministry, especially in souls being saved, and God keeping you in a very hungry and needy place.

> We will remember you this weekend at Doncaster. Do not preach too long. Draw the net before the people are tired. This keeps you fresh, and them also.

Repeat in your heart often, "Baptized with the Holy Ghost and fire, fire, fire!" All the unction, and weeping, and travailing comes through the baptism of fire, and I say to you and say to myself, *purged* and *cleansed* and *filled*, with renewed spiritual power.

God bless you.

His servant,

Smith Wigglesworth

Smith Wigglesworth was unique. He was a commanding figure, finely built with twinkling small eyes in a stout face—rugged and refined at the same time; always immaculately dressed in a dark suit.

It was part of his belief that the Lord looked after His own. I have heard him say that if ever he came to a place where he had less than three decent suits, he would know the Lord wanted him to go back to plumbing.

He was always courteous and kind, and seemed harsh only when he knew he was dealing with satanic forces. Wisdom, brokenness, purity, and spiritual hunger characterized his ministry.

I personally never saw Brother Wigglesworth wear a frown. He was always smiling—never laughing it seemed, but always smiling—and sometimes he had a humorous twinkle in his eyes.

He was a man who knew that his mission was to bless and to edify God's people, to inspire their faith, and to win the lost. He always had a burden on his heart for the sick, the afflicted, and the oppressed.

A Man of One Book

Smith Wigglesworth used to say he would give a five-pound reward to anyone who could catch him, at any time, without either his Bible or his Testament.

I once found he had left his little Testament behind, so I claimed the five pounds. With a smile and a twinkle in his eye, he got out of the challenge by saying he was not without it, but that I happened to pick it up before he did.

I once ventured to offer him a small book to read which had been a blessing to me. He courteously declined, explaining that since the day his wife taught him to read and write, he had never read any book but his Bible.

On that same occasion, referring to the book, he said:

"I couldn't read it; but give it to my son-in-law, Jimmy Salter. He has books all 'round the room to the ceiling.

"When I go to America and sometimes have a time for questions, I answer what I can answer, and when I get one I can't answer, I say, 'My son-in-law, Salter, will answer that. He is a better scholar than I am.'"

When critics asked him how he ever put his first book into print, he replied, "I didn't. Reporters took down those messages, and out came that book!"

Some years before he died, he gave me a copy of the book, which he inscribed with a personal message to me. When giving it to me, he said:

"Now, Brother Hacking, don't lend this book. It's not for lending. If this book is lent, the folks won't buy it, and we want them to buy it. This book has made 20,000 pounds ($50,000) for missionaries."

That was many years ago, and it is still being published and making money for missionaries.

THE FIRST TIME I SAW HIM

My first view of Smith Wigglesworth was from a distance.

A number of us in Blackburn had just come into the Pentecostal experience and were told of a weekend meeting of Evangelist Smith Wigglesworth in Preston. There were not many Pentecostal ministers in the whole of the British Isles in those days. But there were three that were outstanding: Stephen Jeffreys, George Jeffreys, and Smith Wigglesworth.

Smith Wigglesworth was looked upon, even then, as an apostle of faith. With his commanding authority, he had a reputation for being somewhat austere—a "modern Elijah" whose ministry had been attested with phenomenal miracles.

Therefore, it was with great excitement that we looked forward to visiting Preston to hear him. The Assembly room at Preston was situated on Lancaster Road. It was a large room, quite central, but up a dingy stairway of 45 steps. The entrance to this room was uninviting, but week by week and several times during the week, a goodly company of God's people gathered under the godly and inspired leadership of the late Thomas Myerscough.

From time to time, many of the leading people of the Pentecostal testimony from various countries visited this room to minister. It was this Assembly that gave us three outstanding missionary pioneers to the Belgian Congo—Brothers Burton, Salter, and Hodgson—as well as many others who followed them.

So it was on this memorable weeknight that a small company of us (mostly young people for Blackburn) made our way to this "upper room." One of our Blackburn friends at this time was a chronic invalid. She dragged herself around the house slowly by the help of the chairs and the table. Her limbs were hideously swollen. She had not done any housework for years. She was suffering from what the doctors described as a complicated condition of rheumatism, rheumatoid arthritis, neuritis, and bronchitis.

Two or three of us, especially anxious to see her delivered, persuaded her to go to Preston. It was a feat of achievement quite equal to that accomplished by the four friends who got the Paralytic to Jesus. (Mark 2:3.) With the aid of two sticks, it took us three-quarters of an hour to get her from Preston Station to that "upper room," a mere half-mile away. (In those days we could not afford a taxi.)

The meeting began and Brother Wigglesworth started his message. At ten minutes to ten o'clock, he was still preaching a marvelous message on Peter's deliverance from prison. (Acts 12.) Since our train left Preston at 10:15 P.M., we interrupted the preaching to request prayer for our sister.

Brother Wigglesworth laid his hands on her and drastically rebuked the affliction. The next we knew, she was running down the stairs, and we were chasing after her! She was instantly and completely healed!

The next day, she did all her housework. This miracle stirred the neighborhood where she lived and led to the salvation of souls, some becoming earnest members of the young Assembly.

More wonderful still, her husband, a confirmed drunkard on the verge of delirium tremens, came under deep conviction. Two weeks later in the middle of the night, he crawled out of his bed and walked the floor, crying to God for mercy.

In a matter of moments, God wondrously saved him and at the same time, filled him with the Holy Ghost. Like Saul of Tarsus, upon his miraculous and sudden conversion, he joined himself to the disciples and straightway preached Christ. (Acts 9:20,26.) He became the first treasurer of our newly formed Assembly.

This was my first view of Smith Wigglesworth— a view from a distance. Little did I realize that it would be followed by a much closer contact in the days that lay ahead.

This seemed very unlikely at the time, but then the Lord has always been good to me in this respect. As a young man, I was brought into intimate association with some of the great men of

God in the entire Pentecostal movement—all were a constant source of inspiration to me.

He will fulfil the desire of them that fear him....

Psalms 145:19

The strong desire within me then was to have fellowship with the men I had heard so much about—men like Stephen Jeffreys and Smith Wigglesworth. In just a few years' time, that desire was to be fulfilled as I served as co-pastor of a large church with Stephen Jeffreys, and soon after became friends with God's beloved servant, Smith Wigglesworth.

Brother Wigglesworth had a warm place in his heart for young men who were in the ministry. In my first contacts with him, I was in my mid-thirties. It was my privilege and joy to share his company and benefit by his fellowship.

2

Wigglesworth Before the People

Smith Wigglesworth and Thomas Myerscough, the beloved founder of the Preston Assembly, were bosom friends. For all the years that I can remember, Brother Wigglesworth was the invited and honored speaker of the then-famous Preston Annual Pentecostal Convention.

My first visit to the Preston Convention was a memorable one. A number of us young people had cycled from Blackburn and arrived just a little late for the morning service. We went below to the lower schoolroom of the church building and placed our bicycles in the corridor. We could not get our bicycles placed and our coats off fast enough. We were anxious to get into the Convention, which was proceeding in the hall above, where about 500 people were gathered, praising God.

As we entered the Convention hall, it seemed as though everybody in that throng, without exception, was singing "in the Spirit." It was the most amazing harmony I have ever heard. There was absolutely no discord. The voices were blending, and the singing was rising and falling—minor and major, loud and soft. At one moment it seemed to be coming from one side, the next moment from the other side. Then it would rise to a great and wonderful crescendo.

It made us feel that we had arrived at the very portals of the Celestial City.

I think it not an exaggeration to say that this continued for about twenty minutes.

Amazingly, this unified and harmonious singing in tongues was being led by a man standing on the platform, his eyes closed and his hands moving gracefully. He himself would break into the singing at times with the phrase, "Worthy the Lamb."

This songleader, we learned later, was Pastor Jays of Cheltenham, who at that time was a mighty exponent of the Word of God. Several missionaries were seated on the platform.

Thomas Myerscough sat at a portable organ, a special portable "billhorn" that he played under the anointing of the Spirit. One notable adornment to the hall was a large canvas poster, which extended the whole width of the room. On it were inscribed the words: "Not Your Own, *His.*"

Smith Wigglesworth sat at the center of the platform. The impact of his Spirit-filled personality was tremendous. But from all my contact with him, I know there was never a man so utterly oblivious or unconcerned about personality as himself.

The only personality that mattered to Smith Wigglesworth was the Personality of the Holy

Spirit, and the only Person to receive the glory was the Lord Jesus Christ. In fact, he was known to be quite ruthless with anyone attempting to minister, whom he suspected of parading their personality.

WIGGLESWORTH IN WORSHIP

Smith Wigglesworth had the ability to pick up the services from the inception of those great Convention meetings and bring the congregation almost immediately into the Presence of God. He was very clear that there was never to be a staleness in a meeting leading up to a sense of the Presence of God. As far as he was concerned, God was there at the beginning and remained right through to the end.

His methods to many, even in those days, appeared no doubt to be very unorthodox; but they always brought blessing to people who were hungry for God. His exhortations, while leading the people in worship, were often paradoxical and amusing.

He once said: "I want to bring you people to a place of dissatisfaction—a place where you will never be satisfied anymore, only satisfied with an unsatisfiable satisfaction." Another time he said: "Some people are satisfied with it, if it is good; some want it better. The best is only good enough for me improved."

These *Wigglesworthisms* were often accompanied by a message in tongues, given by him and interpreted by a stirring exhortation. What I would call a *Wigglesworthism* was the way he would sing, holding his little Testament on the top of his head: *I know the Lo-o-rd, I know the Lo-o-rd, I know the Lord has laid His hand on me.*

He always concluded by requesting the congregation to lift up their hands and pour out their hearts to the Lord. After several minutes of this congregational worship and prayer, with the people's hands uplifted to the Lord and their faces shining, he would bring the worship and prayer to a close by leading a song.

Often at the close of a service, having gathered the people to the front, he would say, "Come now, I want to help you." Brother Wigglesworth knew that, as the Spirit-filled servant of God, He *could* help them.

Brother Wigglesworth often spoke in tongues during the course of his message. Many times the particular tongue he spoke was sweet and melodious, and led me to think of the words: *The tongues of men and of angels.* (1 Cor. 13:1.) He was a prophet rather than a theologian, and many things he said were unforgettable. For instance: "I would rather have a man on my platform, not filled with the Holy Ghost but hungry for God, than a man who has received the Holy Ghost but has become satisfied with his experience."

An outstanding memory was always Missionary Day at Preston during the Easter Convention under the leadership of Brother Wigglesworth. Great challenges were brought to us by many missionaries, often from many lands. To us young people in those days, Brother Wigglesworth was somewhat of an awesome and mystical figure.

Quite vividly I remember him in a Convention service in Cheetham Street, Preston, as I sat about six or seven seats away from the platform. Sitting there, one's eyes were about level with the platform.

When Brother Wigglesworth started to preach, I noticed a small celluloid anointing bottle, about three inches long and one inch in diameter, lying on the floor of the platform. As Wigglesworth preached, moving to and fro about the platform, his feet would come again and again within an inch of that bottle. But he was totally oblivious of the fact.

Although I was listening to the preaching, I was at the same time watching with curiosity and amazement, expecting him every moment to step on the bottle and crush it, but never once did he touch it. On another occasion, during an Assemblies of God Convention in Sunderland, Wigglesworth was preaching on Pentecost from the familiar portion of Scripture, Acts chapter 2, verses 1-4.

He was describing the tongues of fire coming down from heaven and sitting upon each of them. With hands uplifted above his head, his fingers moving dexterously, he spent a few moments describing this wonderful phenomenon. During the whole of that time, the golden light of the setting sun shone through the windows upon his fingers, making his hands appear to be living flames of fire. Remarkably, when he finished his description of the flames of fire and started to speak on other aspects of the Pentecostal baptism, the sunlight disappeared.

It might well be said that these reflections of mine upon these two incidents are more curious than practical, and I might be willing to agree, but they impressed me with the unerring accuracy with which a man can move when he is moving all the time in the will of God and in the power of the Holy Ghost.

3

Man of Faith and Power

As I have said in chapter 1, in my first contact with Smith Wigglesworth, I was privileged to witness a remarkable miracle of healing when our invalid friend was delivered from the hands of Satan. God wrought this miracle before our very eyes, and the vessel He used was Smith Wigglesworth.

If the many miracles which God wrought by His servant had been collated and recorded, it would provide an extraordinary volume of testimony to the healing power of the Lord Jesus Christ.

Through this beloved servant's ministry over the years, the blind saw, the lame walked, diseases of all kinds were healed, goiters and cancers disappeared, even the dead were raised. (Much could be said, but it is not my purpose to deal at length with the healing ministry of Smith Wigglesworth.)

One of the much-sung hymns in his services was:

All things are possible to him

That can in Jesus' name believe.

And a chorus he was very fond of starting up was "Only Believe."

Predominantly—and I believe we should say characteristically—in Smith Wigglesworth's ministry of healing, he believed in the anointing with oil in obedience to the Word, especially in Mark 6:13:

They ... anointed with oil many that were sick, and healed them.

He had specially manufactured a small celluloid oil bottle for his use. These bottles were sold for a nominal sum and hundreds of them were in use by ministering brethren and others who prayed for the sick. Engraven on the black base were the words:

Wigglesworth, 70 Victor Road, Bradford

It was generally considered that a preacher was only half equipped in those days unless he carried one of these pocket oil bottles.

An Inspiration to Many

There is no doubt that many in the full-time ministry, and out of it, were inspired by Brother Wigglesworth's faith and example. There were some who copied him in method, in manner, and even in voice. This should not be considered so much a charge against them as a testimony to the towering character of this truly grand personality.

I can personally confess that I was never in the company of Smith Wigglesworth for five minutes without feeling within me a great surge of inspiration to believe God.

For me to look today at his photograph—see the smile, the twinkling eyes, the calm serenity reflected on his countenance—brings to me once again a fresh inspiration, even after all these years.

Brother Wigglesworth not only prayed for the deliverance of others, but he was strong in faith for his own deliverance. I have heard him say publicly, "I do not know that I have a body."

An excellent example of this was shared during a Preston Convention service by Dr. Lanz, a famous dental surgeon from Switzerland. Dr. Lanz told of his first encounter with Brother Wigglesworth. It was at a large gathering in Switzerland where Wigglesworth was preaching and ministering to the sick.

At that time Brother Wigglesworth was at least seventy years of age, and I think about seventy-five. Dr. Lanz, who had not at that time come into this glorious full salvation, challenged Brother Wigglesworth from the floor of the building. He said, "Mr. Wigglesworth, you are preaching divine healing. Why could not God have preserved your teeth so that you would not have to wear false teeth?"

In reply, Wigglesworth said, "If anybody in this audience—or you, sir—can after this service discover that these teeth are not my own, but false, there is a five-pound reward for him."

Dr. Lanz was not to be deceived. He went into the vestry. There to his amazement he found that Brother Wigglesworth did not have false teeth. They were his own and like new.

TRIUMPH OVER SICKNESS

In later years, however, Wigglesworth's faith in God for healing was to pass through a severe trial. For three years he suffered agony with the extremely excruciating affliction of gallstones. When informed by a specialist that the only way of deliverance was an operation, Wigglesworth said, "God shall operate."

His son-in-law, James Salter, told me that during this time they paid a visit to United States together, preaching almost nightly. Brother Wigglesworth was in much pain and bled a great deal. He spent his days in bed, went by taxi each night to the meetings, then immediately went back to bed. This went on, day after day and night after night.

"Yet," said Brother Salter, "those meetings were marvelous—great messages from Brother Wigglesworth, attended with great spiritual power, and attested by wonderful miracles of God's healing power."

When deliverance came to Brother Wigglesworth, it was mighty! Almost instantaneously, all the gallstones, twenty or more, came away; and Brother Wigglesworth was perfectly whole. He put those stones in a small tin, and on one occasion he showed them to me. Some were quite large; others were jagged and needle-shaped. All were capable of not only giving intense pain, but of penetrating deeply, hence the constant hemorrhages.

Smith Wigglesworth had occasionally suffered minor ailments, but he always came forth with the same note of victory. In a letter to me upon his recovery from a more prolonged attack, he said:

"The Lord has marvelously quickened me according to Romans 8:11, *If the Spirit of him that raised up Jesus from the dead dwell in you, he that raised up Christ from the dead shall also quicken your mortal bodies by his Spirit that dwelleth in you.*"

Brother Wigglesworth not only exemplified a living faith, but he also entertained a shrewd and wise approach to everything. He took care of himself.

More than once after a meeting, I have helped him put on one cardigan after another, while he remarked in a knowing way to me: "Always keep warm, Brother Hacking. If you feel cold, put more on. Never mind what folks think or say."

Remarkably enough, although Brother Wigglesworth was so truly an apostle of faith, he knew his own limitations, or perhaps it would be better to say, as he has said, he knew his "particular line of faith."

He once sent me a large report on the Swansea Bible College and the record of how Rees Howells prayed in 100,000 pounds. Included was his remark: "Read this, Brother Hacking. It will increase your faith. This does not seem to be my particular line of faith." This I thought was very remarkable in Brother Wigglesworth, and probably helps throw some light on the last clause in Romans 12, verse 3: ... *God hath dealt to every man the measure of faith.*

In the case of Smith Wigglesworth, I have always felt that, while some of us talk about faith and try to define it, he was the living embodiment of this great gift of Grace.

4

Man of Love

One could never think of Smith Wigglesworth without thinking of Bradford. Though I was never in the Bowland Street Mission of which he was the leader, I did pay periodic visits to his home at 70 Victor Road there in Bradford. It was a rather big rambling house, but to Brother Wigglesworth it was "Home, Sweet Home."

Some people have an image of Smith Wigglesworth as a man aloof, apart, and difficult to approach. It might surprise them to know that he loved fellowship.

During the days when I pastored the Royston Church, some twenty miles from Bradford,

Brother Wigglesworth would oftentimes send me my fare to come and pay him a visit. These visits were always a precious memory.

Smith Wigglesworth was simple, homely, and always seemed to impart something of the life of God. When one such visit was coming to an end, he put his hand on my shoulder and said, "You will have to be going, Brother Hacking, so we will pray."

That prayer I have never forgotten, for its grandeur and its brevity. He said, "Lord, give us, Thy servants, great searchings of heart, great decisions of will, and great assurances through the blood of Jesus. Amen." Then quite abruptly he said, "Now, Brother Hacking, you will have to be away to get your bus, or else you will miss the train."

One minute in heaven; the next minute on earth.

Spirituality plus practicability.

Smith Wigglesworth was always a wonderful combination of the two.

It is a well-known common saying that you can be so heavenly minded as to be no earthly good. I have always maintained, too, that you can be so earthly minded as to be no heavenly good.

God's servant, Smith Wigglesworth, always impressed me as striking the balance exactly, combining at all times deep spirituality with sensible practicability.

For many years, the Bradford Convention attracted an increasing number of hungry saints and visitors. Brother Wigglesworth was not only the host and the leader, but an example as well to the people in hospitality. In his words:

"Our house was always crammed with visitors to the Convention. Not only have they been sleeping in every available bed, but also in the bathroom, and on the floor.

On one occasion when we were already overcrowded with visitors, a man knocked on the door and asked to be accommodated so that he could attend the services of the Convention. I could not deny that brother.

"The man was delighted that he was permitted to stay with us. However, he made one strange request. He said, 'I have one request to make of you, Brother Wigglesworth. When you are having your meals, will you please give me only dry bread and water? For many years, this has been my only diet. If I was given more, I could not eat it.'

"Without a doubt," said Brother Wigglesworth, "I never saw a man who was more a picture of health as he was. Later I asked a chemist about this and he said, 'Then that was supernatural. In the natural, that man, with bread and water alone, was not being supplied with sufficient nourishment to keep him alive.' We are reminded of the promise: *The Lord shall bless thy bread and water.*" (Ex. 23:25.)

As leader of the Bowland Street Mission, Brother Wigglesworth was led on one occasion to observe literally Jesus' words in Luke 14:13,14:

But when thou makest a feast, call the poor, the maimed, the lame, the blind:

And thou shalt be blessed; for they cannot recompense thee: for thou shalt be recompensed at the resurrection of the just.

Brother Wigglesworth made one requirement of those who came to that meal: They must be willing to listen to a short Gospel message. Many came, and on that occasion the worst man in Bradford was saved. When Brother Wigglesworth related to me the character of this man, I had no doubt in my mind that he was indeed the worst man in Bradford.

Smith Wigglesworth was a gracious, considerate man of wise character. His true shepherdly care always stands out to me in a statement he made concerning his leadership of the open-air meetings in connection with the Bradford Mission. He said:

"In cold weather, when we used to hold an open-air service, I would always put on the thinnest suit I had and wear the thinnest pair of shoes I could find. I knew there would be some standing there who were not as well clothed as I was. In this way I could have an idea that when I was beginning to feel cold, they were, and it was time to close the meeting."

This wise and compassionate consideration has helped me on more than one occasion in dealing with others, to be considerate rather than demanding.

When you had the opportunity of more intimate contact with Smith Wigglesworth, you knew that he was not only the possessor of a living faith, but that it was always a *faith which worketh by love* (Gal. 5:6).

Those who heard him minister from time to time will bear witness that as he preached and as he ministered to the sick, the tears would be trickling down his cheeks. Broken in spirit as he was, the brokenness oftentimes would sweep over the whole congregation.

Smith Wigglesworth was a skillful personal soulwinner. He tells how on board ship on one voyage across the Atlantic, a concert was arranged. He was approached and asked to take part.

"Well," he said, "on one condition, that you put me down first on the program to sing." That apparently was quite agreeable. The concert began, and he was introduced as the first artist.

No doubt before he went to that concert, he had prayed much. I do not recollect whether there were any immediate conversions as a result, but the sense of God's Presence was so felt that some were in tears, and it was impossible to continue the concert.

No doubt an impression was made upon many that would remain to their dying day.

Brother Wigglesworth, like Charles Finney, believed that the presence of a man filled with

God could bring conviction to sinners without even a word being spoken. As he sat opposite a man in a railway carriage, the man suddenly jumped up, exclaimed, "You convict me of sin!" and went out into another carriage.

5

Set Apart for God

Like most of God's true servants, there are sides of character known to the public and sides not known to the public. There is great wealth of character in any true servant of God. To interpret him from only one angle is to do a great injustice. (See 2 Cor. 6:1-10.) This was true of Smith Wigglesworth.

"DIVINE AUDACITY"

Many who remember him, even to this day, think of him as abrupt, perhaps even hard and somewhat unapproachable. He certainly was a unique character. There could not be another like him. It could well be that in the earlier years, his sense of calling—his feeling of the need for what he called "divine audacity"—made him seem sometimes abrupt.

How well I remember being with him for a convention in Yorkshire. We had a morning free, and our host took us for a drive through the Dukeries—a luxuriant stretch of countryside situated somewhere on the border between Yorkshire and Nottinghamshire. Our conversation (as always when Smith Wigglesworth was involved) was of a high standard and centered around the deep things of God.

Suddenly, however, in quite a different strain, he said, "How would you like to go to America, Brother Hacking?"

I replied, "I should like very much to go if it was in the will of God for me, but I would not want to go, any more than you would, unless it was clearly the will of God."

"Well, that's right," he said.

I continued, "However, it wouldn't be much use my thinking about going to America unless I had somebody like yourself to recommend me."

"You don't need my recommendation," he said. "That wouldn't be any use."

Then he told me the most fantastic story of how he first went to America. He said, "The only thing is to know the will of God, to know the Lord has called you to go, and then go."

He went on: "When I first went, I knew the Lord wanted me to go. He put on my heart the campmeeting he wanted me to go to. I procured my passport, my travel ticket, and made sure my family would be fully provided for during the three months I was away. If any provide not for his own, he has denied the faith, and is worse than an infidel. (1 Tim. 5:8.) And then I went."

When he arrived at the campmeeting, he was refused the opportunity to speak. The convention chairman explained: "It is impossible. Our platform of speakers is arranged for months before the convention takes place." But that was nothing to this Apostle of Faith. Wigglesworth knew that if God had sent him, He would make a way for him to speak. And He did!

God blessed that first message, and His saving grace and healing power were displayed. How Wigglesworth was invited back for further ministry is a story of miraculous overruling and intervention.

In those earlier years, his method of praying for the sick was considered rough by some. But he viewed all sickness as the oppression of the devil, and his belief was, "You can't deal with the devil gently." He felt he had to deal drastically with the devil behind the sickness; yet at the same time, his heart was filled with overflowing compassion for the sick one.

If he had prayed for a person, he would say, "The next thing is to believe God."

To one dear woman who came to him in the healing line for prayer, he said, "What's the matter with you?"

"It's my heart," she replied.

"Weren't you here for prayer yesterday?"

"Yes."

"Well, what's the matter now?"

"My heart."

Giving her a gentle push, he said, "Go away with you, woman, and believe God. There's nothing the matter with your heart. It's your faith."

Because of the unfortunate idea that Brother Wigglesworth might deal with them roughly or make a show of them, some people were afraid to come forward for healing in his meetings. Yet of those who did, so many were wonderfully healed. Many through the years have testified to me of how they were miraculously healed in one of Brother Wigglesworth's meetings.

A rather amusing incident was related to me in this connection. Two young ministers, who had been dining out together during one of the conventions, were both suffering from pain in the stomach, so they came forward for healing. As they took their place in the healing line, there was a woman standing between them.

Wigglesworth came to the first young man and asked the familiar question, "Well, brother, what's the matter with you?"

"Stomach pain."

Wigglesworth said, "Close your eyes." Then he commanded, "In the name of Jesus, come out of him!" He struck the man in the stomach, sending him halfway across the front of the hall. Then he stepped over to the woman who was next in line. Amazingly, he prayed with her quite simply and gently.

As Wigglesworth approached the other young minister, who had watched as his friend was struck so forcefully, he asked, "What's the matter with you, brother?"

The young man replied, sheepishly, "Headache."

COMPASSION FOR THE SICK

Smith Wigglesworth had a great compassion for the sick and suffering. He would take the sick as a burden to his heart and pray diligently for them. Day after day, requests came to him from all over the world, asking for prayer. He would place these upon his list and take them upon his heart. Many answers to those prayer requests are on record.

Quite unsolicited on one occasion, when I had suffered from duodenal ulcers for many years, Brother Wigglesworth sent me an anointed hand-kerchief. He told me that he had been burdened with my condition and instructed me to lay it on the affected part and to believe God.

PREACHING THE FAITH OF JESUS

One of Wigglesworth's great convictions was that faith was creative: *What God can do, He does for faith. All things are possible with God. All things are possible to him that believeth.* (Mark 9:23).

One of his favorite Scriptures, and one which I heard him quote so often, was Mark 11:23:

For verily I say unto you, That whosoever shall say unto this mountain, Be thou removed, and be thou cast into the sea; and shall not doubt in his heart, but shall believe that those things which he saith shall come to pass; he shall have whatsoever he saith.

He always made a point of emphasizing the phrase, *Whatsoever he SAITH*—not what we *pray for* or *hope for*, but *saith*. He not only preached the importance of faith, but he exalted Jesus and made Jesus so real and present and wonderful that somehow it was easy to believe.

42

6

He Walked With God

Smith Wigglesworth had a habit, even in his eighties, of taking about a half-hour's walk each morning and each afternoon—and all the better if the countryside was close at hand.

If you took a walk with Brother Wigglesworth, whether in town or in country, you had to be prepared to stop on the way many times and pray with him.

On that walk you would probably stop about six times while Brother Wigglesworth took hold of your hands, lifted his eyes to heaven, and prayed. It would be just a few simple sentences. Then you would walk a little farther.

Like Enoch, Wigglesworth walked and talked with God, and he didn't ask anyone's permission to do so. Needless to say, when you took a walk with him, his conversation was always about the things of God. You were helped, inspired, edified—a better man because of it.

There were times when Brother Wigglesworth was visiting that my activities made it difficult for me to take a walk every day, both morning and afternoon. During one of these times, some of the fine young men in our Assembly asked if perhaps they might go with him instead of me.

When I mentioned this to him, he was delighted. He always took great pleasure in being able to help young men in the things of God. During the course of the walk, he said, "Now, if you young men want to ask me any questions about anything, just go ahead."

One of them said, "Mr. Wigglesworth, how can one come to possess great faith?"

Replied Wigglesworth: "Now, listen, here is the answer to that: *First the blade, then the ear, after that the full corn in the ear* (Mark 4:28). Faith must grow by soil, moisture, and exercise." Those young men, on fire for God and souls, never forgot his unique answer.

A Bold Witness

A fear of man was foreign to Smith Wigglesworth. At the close of one of his visits to Blackburn, about thirty of the Assembly members gathered at the station to see him off. With about fifteen minutes to spare before the train came in, Wigglesworth wasted no time. He said, "Let's go into the waiting room."

When we were all in and settled, he led us in song and in prayer. Then he shared a work of exhortation, bringing to a conclusion a wonderful unscheduled service on a railway station platform. There were a number of lookers-on, and they must have been tremendously impressed.

Smith Wigglesworth no doubt was thoroughly familiar with Paul's words: Buy up the opportunities for *the days are evil* (Eph. 5:16). He was always courteous, but always bold.

OBLIVIOUS TO CIRCUMSTANCES

A quiet calm always seemed to mark Smith Wigglesworth's attitude under all circumstances. I have just referred to his habit of taking walks regularly. When I pastored Royston Assembly, I lived in a bungalow in Meadow Lane. That lane the postman knew as "Glory Row." Twenty-seven of our Assembly lived in that lane.

Brother Wigglesworth was staying in the next bungalow to ours. Less than a stone's throw away at our back door was the canal.

One blustery morning we started up the lane for the usual short walk. Brother Wigglesworth, getting on in years, walked slowly with measured steps. Turning left at the end of the lane, we climbed a steep incline in the road, which brought us to a humpback bridge spanning the canal.

The wind was blowing things in all directions. Brother Wigglesworth was always immaculately dressed, and this particular morning he was wearing a smart new cap, which obviously had cost quite a bit of money. Just as we reached the summit of the bridge, a great gust of wind lifted his new cap and blew it off his head and into the canal.

I have often said that if that cap had been mine, I would have been diving into the canal to retrieve it. Not Brother Wigglesworth.

Without turning an eyelid, he quietly turned 'round and said, "We had better go back, Brother Hacking. I can't go walking out on a day like this without a cap on my head." Perfect calm. Smith Wigglesworth knew a place in God where nothing disturbed him. He could say with Paul, *None of these things move me* (Acts 20:24).

A MAN OF GENEROSITY

Not only did Smith Wigglesworth give a great deal to missionary work, he gave wherever he felt there was a need. On many occasions when small churches had given him all they could afford for his services, he gave it back to them. This fact about Smith Wigglesworth is very little known, but I know it to be true.

On one occasion when the convention costs at Kingsway were twenty pounds in the "red" (and that was quite a bit of money in those days!), Brother Wigglesworth not only took nothing for his own services, but out of his own pocket footed the bill.

Yet in spite of these things, there were wild rumors that he would not minister in any church unless they could guarantee him a certain amount.

There was one county in the North where I ministered quite often in those days, but Brother Wigglesworth had never once been invited there.

The sole reason was the people had heard the rumors that were abroad and were under the impression that he required a financial guarantee for his services. While staying with one of these pastors, a godly brother, I asked, "Why don't you invite Smith Wigglesworth?"

"Oh, brother," he said, "we can't afford to have Brother Wigglesworth."

"Why?"

Then he related these rumors to me. I said, "Brother, it is a very serious matter that you as a district are keeping such a servant of God out of your churches. You are robbing your people of the benefits of an anointed ministry, which could bring great blessing to many. And why? Because you are listening to rumors, which you have not taken the trouble to thoroughly investigate. I know them to be totally unfounded."

When I gave this brother the truth of the matter, he was very sorry. Almost immediately, he invited Brother Wigglesworth and opened a door of ministry that had been closed for years.

7

Wigglesworth—The Preacher

If you did not have the privilege of hearing Smith Wigglesworth preach, you will have to wait until you get to heaven to know what it was like. I do not recollect ever hearing any other preacher quite like him. I had heard great preachers, eloquent preachers—both Pentecostal and non-Pentecostal as far as denomination is concerned—but Wigglesworth was out on his own.

He had no homiletics, but he certainly had dynamics. When I say dynamics, I do not mean that he was vociferous or boiterous. Actually, there was always a poise, a reverence, a dignity of demeanor in his presentation.

Many of his sentences were abstract, often disconnected, sometimes enigmatical, sometimes even ungrammatical, but often pithy. For example, he said, "Some like to read their Bible in Hebrew. Some like to read their Bible in Greek. I prefer to read mine in the Holy Ghost."

For the most part, however, his sentences were filled with inspiration and revelation. The hearer was edified, inspired, changed. One sentence sometimes was like a sermon, capable of changing the course of your life. For example:

"Any man can be changed by faith," or "Never say, 'I can't' if you are filled with the Holy Ghost."

The whole secret was that these were words from the lips of a man who was in close touch with God—a man on fire for God.

8

Notes on His Preaching

While I was pastoring the church in Royston, Brother Wigglesworth visited us for a week of meetings. I cannot write shorthand, but I took extensive longhand notes of all his messages that week. These notes mostly represent his terse sayings. Second rate as I felt the notes to be, I well remember how pleased Brother Wigglesworth was to have them recorded. It is the record of these sentences that will form the substance of this final and considerably longer chapter.

When presented in their original form, my introduction to these notes was as follows: "What a joy it has been for us to have a visit from God's servant. We have had one week only, but it has been a week of heaven—a week in the Presence of God. What a fragrance has rested upon not only the messages that have been given from the platform, but the private conversations and exhortations of His servant.

"The lost have found Christ. The sick have been healed. But perhaps more than everything else, the Living Word has been magnified. Jesus has been made Wonderful.

"The following represents the gist of the messages brought to us, which I trust will bring revelation, profit, and increase to all who read."

JESUS REMOVED THE "IF"

When he was come down from the mountain, great multitudes followed him.

And, behold, there came a leper and worshipped him, saying, Lord, if thou wilt, thou canst make me clean.

And Jesus put forth his hand, and touched him, saying, I will; be thou clean. And immediately his leprosy was cleansed.

And Jesus saith unto him, See thou tell no man; but go thy way, shew thyself to the priest, and offer the gift that Moses commanded, for a testimony unto them.

And Jesus saith unto him, The foxes have holes, and the birds of the air have nests; but the Son of man hath not where to lay his head.

Matthew 8:1-4,20

Here we have the good and the helpless, the mighty and the needy.

So helpless was this leper when he came to Jesus!

God can't help you whilst you can help yourself.

Jesus ... Oh, isn't that a wonderful Name!

How the outlook changes when Jesus comes!

Jesus knew this leper would come to Him.

My Lord went at night to talk to the Father. In communication of the night, the program of the next day was worked out between Him and the Father.

As Jesus was coming down from the mountain, He was filled with glory and every eye was fixed on Him. The people were so interested in watching Jesus coming down from the Glory that the leper, unknown to the people, had gotten through.

When the people saw him, they gave him plenty of room; so he got to the feet of Jesus.

This leper, like many who are in need today, knew that Jesus could. But they doubt His *willingness*. Jesus wanted to remove the "if" for all generations to come by His words, "I will."

Foxes have holes, and the birds of the air have nests; but the Son of man hath not where to lay his head. (Luke 9:58.) Did you ever think why, with so many loving husbands and wives about, and many who would have just loved to have had Him, Jesus was not invited?

Is not the simple answer that He would see too much?

Those burning eyes of His would see everything! So the people were afraid to have Him.

POWER FROM ON HIGH

Until the day in which he was taken up, after that he through the Holy Ghost had given commandments unto the apostles whom he had chosen:

And, being assembled together with them, commanded them that they should not depart from Jerusalem, but wait for the promise of the Father, which, saith he, ye have heard of me.

For John truly baptized with water; but ye shall be baptized with the Holy Ghost not many days hence.

But ye shall receive power, after that the Holy Ghost is come upon you: and ye shall be witnesses unto me both in Jerusalem, and in all

Judaea, and in Samaria, and unto the utter-
most part of the earth.

Acts 1:2,4-5,8

And Jesus looking upon them saith, With men
it is impossible, but not with God: for with
God all things are possible.

Mark 10:27

You will have to voice many things in order to
bring them into being.

God wants us to have great faith.

My wife and I had nine children, but it didn't
matter which one cried in the street; my wife
knew who it was. God will come to the one who
cries first.

I want to help you decide that, by the power of
God, you will not be ordinary.

If you are in the same place today as you were
yesterday, you are a backslider.

One thing in these verses we must not forget: The love of Jesus. He wanted them to carry on the work exactly as He had done it.

If they had awakened to the Resurrection Position, they would never have done what they did—all go fishing. God allowed everything to fail. He wanted every one of them to be excelsior.

You have to have a clothing that is not made on earth. Your whole nature has to have a clothing of all righteousness.

It is an insult to ask God for power after you have received the baptism of the Holy Ghost. You *have* power! You have to *act*!

Tongues and interpretation: "Power from on high.... It is God inserting into you divine activity with mightiness."

I am always on my merit. Every time I preach, I preach my best. Every time I pray, I pray my best.

Jesus began His ministry everywhere by His miraculous Manifestation; then they all pressed upon Him to hear. He was the First-fruits.

We have to step into line of the First-fruits. God *makes* the opportunity. We have to *take* the opportunity. We can live so that the opportunity is always occurring.

Unless we are ready to do the impossible, we will never come into "maternity" (bring other souls to the birth).

God has said that impossibilities are with men but that possibilities are with God.

Are you living in God or in man? In opposition? Or is it all opportunity?

To the man of faith, there is not a thing that is not opportunity.

If you can be fascinated by anything else in the world, you don't have what God wants you to have.

I am all Pentecost.

You have to bring your mind to the Word of God and not try to bring the Word of God to your mind.

FAITH—OUR INHERITANCE

Now faith is the substance of things hoped for, the evidence of things not seen.

For by it the elders obtained a good report.

Through faith we understand that the worlds were framed by the word of God, so that things which are seen were not made of things which do appear.

By faith Abel offered unto God a more excellent sacrifice than Cain, by which he obtained witness that he was righteous, God testifying of his gifts: and by it he being dead yet speaketh.

By faith Enoch was translated that he should not see death; and was not found, because God had translated him: for before his translation he had this testimony, that he pleased God.

But without faith it is impossible to please him: for he that cometh to God must believe that he is, and that he is a rewarder of them that diligently seek him.

By faith Noah, being warned of God of things not seen as yet, moved with fear, prepared an ark to the saving of his house; by the which he condemned the world, and became heir of the righteousness which is by faith.

By faith Abraham, when he was called to go out into a place which he should after receive for an inheritance, obeyed; and he went out, not knowing whither he went.

By faith he sojourned in the land of promise, as in a strange country, dwelling in tabernacles with Isaac and Jacob, the heirs with him of the same promise:

For he looked for a city which hath foundations, whose builder and maker is God.

Hebrews 11:1-10

There are wonderful things right in the very midst of us when we are ready to receive them.

Without faith, you have nothing. You cannot be saved without it. You cannot be healed without it.

If you make a stop between Calvary and the Glory, you miss a great deal. Always have something which is better.

You say, "What makes you so full of inspiration and faith?"

The answer: "Because it is from faith to faith."

After you have once laid hold of the plan on the lines of faith—the simplicity of faith—you will be in a new world.

There is such a thing as talking about faith without using it as an inheritance.

(At this juncture, he told us about a woman who wrote to him in great distress, saying, "Can you help me?" Her letter was full of Scripture and wonderful truth. Brother Wigglesworth sent the letter back to her and wrote underneath: "Believe your own letter." She did and was wonderfully delivered!)

You have to examine yourself tonight to see whether you are *in the faith* or only *talking faith*.

The baptism of the Holy Ghost has brought us to the fact of a remarkable Personality dwelling within us, which is all faith.

The New Birth is God in the life. God's Word lives! It is the only Book that has eternal power in every line. You will lose out if you put aside this Book for any other.

You must have the Word of God abiding in you if you want faith to be in evidence.

Faith doesn't take any strength to carry—it carries you.

It doesn't matter how you are clothed as a believer—if you haven't got the Word of God in your pocket, you are not properly dressed.

You are born again of the Incorruptible Word. Then there is within you the Word that can change everything that is in the world. But not if you waver!

ACTING IN FAITH

Therefore I say unto you, What things soever ye desire, when ye pray, believe that ye receive them, and ye shall have them.

And when ye stand praying, forgive, if ye have aught against any: that your Father also which is in heaven may forgive you your trespasses.

Mark 11:24,25

If there is anything in your heart which is in the way of condemnation, you cannot pray the prayer of faith.

Purity is vital to faith.

The most staggering condition of helplessness which could ever be brought before you is your chance for God to use you.

How is faith received? By acting on that which you have. If you act with what you have, your faith will be increased. You can never increase faith until you act.

KEEPING THE DEVIL IN CHECK

And Jesus being full of the Holy Ghost returned from Jordan, and was led by the Spirit into the wilderness,

Being forty days tempted of the devil. And in those days he did eat nothing: and when they were ended, he afterward hungered.

And Jesus answered and said unto him, Get thee behind me, Satan: for it is written, Thou shalt worship the Lord thy God, and him only shalt thou serve.

The Spirit of the Lord is upon me, because he hath anointed me to preach the gospel to the poor; he hath sent me to heal the broken-hearted, to preach deliverance to the captives, and recovering of sight to the blind, to set at liberty them that are bruised,

To preach the acceptable year of the Lord.

Luke 4:1-2,8,18-19

If you want to increase in the life of God, then you must settle it in your heart that you will not at any time resist the Holy Spirit.

The Holy Ghost and fire—the fire burning up everything that would impoverish and destroy you.

Oh, to be so laid hold of by the Holy Ghost that you have no choice. You have your choice, but you won't choose. God must choose for you.

When Jesus contested the devil in the wilderness, all the demon powers, the wild beasts, and all that was in the wilderness had the vision of the most beautiful Man who ever lived.

The devil always comes to try you in your weakness, but we should not forget that we are stronger in our weakness than in our strength if we dare believe.

I don't come onto this platform with an arrangement of what I have to say, because I have an arrangement with the Father to say what He wants me to say.

There are "thoughts of evil" and "evil thoughts." Spirit and flesh never unite. Holiness and sin never touch each other. The man who hates sin is always in power.

Jesus had so much that was better than what the devil could offer Him.

Love not the world. If you find your mind once diverted from the mind of Christ, repent. It is a clear principle that if you *fall* down, the Angel will lift you up. If you *throw* yourself down, he won't.

We are always to have the devil in check.

The best thing that you ever could have is a great trial. It is your "robing time." It is your coming into inheritance.

Voice your position in God and you will be surrounded by all the resources of God in the time of trial.

Shout, "Get thee behind me, Satan," and you will have the best time on earth. Whisper it, and you won't.

We miss the grandeur because we lack audacity. Greater is He that is within you than he that is in the world. (1 John 4:4.) If you will voice God at any time, you will find that He will be greater than any power that is round about you.

In regard to reading the Scriptures: When you read a Scripture that doesn't fit into the atmosphere and you don't understand it, pass it on to others that are there, that are in accord with the atmosphere that you find yourself in.

If you want a great blessing, always pray first in every meeting. What has that got to do with it? *Everything*. If you pray first, you may have a chance to pray again.

If you see anybody discouraged, get to know the reason of that discouragement and help that person out.

Wise believers always pray short prayers in a public meeting but a long time at home.

When the Church of God is alive in prayer and alive in testimony, the people will come a long way to hear that.

LIFE IN THE SPIRIT

For the law of the Spirit of life in Christ Jesus hath made me free from the law of sin and death.

For they that are after the flesh do mind the things of the flesh; but they that are after the Spirit the things of the Spirit.

For to be carnally minded is death; but to be spiritually minded is life and peace.

Because the carnal mind is enmity against God: for it is not subject to the law of God, neither indeed can be.

So then they that are in the flesh cannot please God.

Therefore, brethren, we are debtors, not to the flesh, to live after the flesh.

Romans 8:2,5-8,12

Every meeting provides an advantage, an open door for us to come deeper into the life of God. But it is possible to be in a wonderful meeting and miss God's purpose through inactivity of faith or lack of submission to the Divine Will.

Perfect peace is God's gift, but our minds stayed on Him is our responsibility. (Isa. 26:3.) Always have within you the knowledge that you are acting on the Word of God. You cannot depend on feelings or on what you see or on anything else. Have no confidence in anything which is on a natural plane.

This Eighth of Romans is a great summit of Divine Truth. If you can only get into this chapter, you will be sin-proof and devil-proof.

Christ in you. (Col. 1:27.) There is a greater power within you than anything that is in the world. (1 John 4:4.)

You must claim the position that your whole body be kept in the place of purity. Christ within you is greater than any carnal power. If you will use your voice, you have a right to rebuke carnality.

Exactly as Christ was created in Mary, so in us. The seed has to produce the manifestation of the sons of God.

There is a life within your life, a mind within your mind, a law of God ruling within your mortal body.

You must never give way because you are tempted and tested, for God chastens His own. If He did not chasten us, it would indicate that we were bastards and not sons, but He chastens you that you shall share His holiness.

God has clothed us with the Spirit of revelation that we may know what we are born out of and into in due time. What is heaven below but a condescension of Jesus in the human flesh?

I want to move you to a greater hunger for holiness and purity. The moment you look up when you are in the place of affection with the Lord Jesus, the heavens are opened.

Whatever has happened in my life up to this moment is of no importance. What matters is what God is to me now.

We have power to put into a helpless place the deeds of the body, and by this means, we begin to live in the Spirit. All the glory is centered in that lovely Jesus because of a yielded will.

PARTAKING OF HIS DIVINE NATURE

Simon Peter, a servant and an apostle of Jesus Christ, to them that have obtained like precious faith with us through the righteousness of God and our Savior Jesus Christ:

Grace and peace be multiplied unto you through the knowledge of God, and of Jesus our Lord,

According as his divine power hath given unto us all things that pertain unto life and godliness, through the knowledge of him that hath called us to glory and virtue:

Whereby are given unto us exceeding great and precious promises: that by these ye might be partakers of the divine nature, having escaped the corruption that is in the world through lust.

And besides this, giving all diligence, add to your faith virtue; and to virtue knowledge;

And to knowledge temperance; and to temperance patience; and to patience godliness;

And to godliness brotherly kindness; and to brotherly kindness charity.

For if these things be in you, and abound, they make you that ye shall neither be barren nor unfruitful in the knowledge of our Lord Jesus Christ.

But he that lacketh these things is blind, and cannot see afar off, and hath forgotten that he was purged from his old sins.

Wherefore the rather, brethren, give diligence to make your calling and election sure: for if ye do these things, ye shall never fall:

**For so an entrance shall be ministered unto
you abundantly into the everlasting kingdom
of our Lord and Savior Jesus Christ.**

2 Peter 1:1-11

You cannot have a holy thought from the
human nature.

God's plan for you is to forget the past in every
way, because the future is so amazingly wonderful.
Oh, the Word of God is so wonderful! This Word so
eats me up that I have no place but in God's Word.

Like precious faith.

The righteousness of God.

*His divine power hath given unto us all things
that pertain unto life and godliness.*

Exceeding great and precious promises.

We have escaped the corruption that is in
the world.

Giving diligence, add to your faith.

... entrance ... into the ... kingdom.

This is the life of God in us—what it means to be partakers of the Divine Nature!

TRADING FLESH FOR SPIRIT

What shall we say then that Abraham our father, as pertaining to the flesh, hath found?

Romans 4:1

What had God for that flesh? Abraham was as good as dead and Sarah about the same.

What has God for that flesh?

The answer is *everything!* We are natural, and very much so, but God has everything for that flesh.

What had God?

The answer is *quickening, Isaac, resurrection.*

I never seek what to say on the platform because when the Holy Ghost has come, we have to be prophetic. I believe in being absorbed by the power of the Holy Ghost. I am on the plan of daring, acting in the Holy Ghost.

This meeting was arranged before the world began, and we are in the design of God.

The plan of God for our life is that you should be held captive by His power, doing that which you in the natural would never do, but that which you are forced to do by the power of the Holy Ghost moving through you.

Everyone in this place who is saved has a million times more than they know. All things are possible—only believe. That is all.

I reckon that the moment you believe, grace is multiplied because you act in faith. You want peace, and God's plan is to multiply peace: *Grace and peace be multiplied unto you* (1 Pet. 1:2).

Peace like a river—undisturbed by anything—this is your inheritance. If you had ten million pounds at your disposal, you could not buy it. It comes to the broken and contrite heart—the heart that says an inward *amen* to God and will not withdraw that *amen* for anything.

I want you to promise the Lord that, from tonight, you will not think back, look back, or act back!

Epilogue

A Life on fire, a life ablaze with God,
Lighted by fire of Pentecostal Love.
A Life on fire, on fire with love for souls,
Lit by Divine compassion from above.

Baptize each one with fire, most Blessed Lord.
Oh, turn us into burning ones in Thee.
Oh, set our hearts ablaze, Thou God of fire,
And let the world Thy Great Salvation see.

These lines, I feel, are an appropriate summing up of the life that we have been considering together. The life of Smith Wigglesworth was *a life on fire—a life ablaze with God.*

There was nothing intermittent about Smith Wigglesworth's consecration. His fire was ever burning on the altar: *The fire shall ever be burning upon the altar; it shall never go out* (Lev. 6:13). That fire was Pentecostal Love.

There was no compromise in Brother Wigglesworth. He had burned all his bridges behind him. Moreover, anybody having anything to do with him, even to converse with him, would feel that they were being searched through and through. He was a living embodiment of the Word in Hebrews chapter 4, verses 12 and 13:

> For the word of God is quick, and powerful, and sharper than any twoedged sword, piercing even to the dividing asunder of soul and spirit, and of the joints and marrow, and is a discerner of the thoughts and intents of the heart.
>
> Neither is there any creature that is not manifest in his sight: but all things are naked and opened unto the eyes of him with whom we have to do.

Smith Wigglesworth was on fire with love for souls, and God used him in the salvation of many. And there was no doubt that his soul was lit by divine compassion. To those who were observant, it is no exaggeration to say that, like the great

Apostle to the Gentiles, Brother Wigglesworth served the Lord *with all humility of mind, and with many tears.* (Acts 20:19.)

Smith Wigglesworth died at the altar, serving his Lord. Two weeks later, I was standing in the vestry on the spot where he died. The Elder, Brother Hibbert, who had been present at the time, described it this way:

"He was standing there. He stood with his back to the fire, warming his hands; it was a cold winter's day. He had just asked me, 'Brother Hibbert, how is your daughter whom I prayed for a few months ago?' I was just about to reply, but he was gone—gone into the Presence of his Lord."

Prayer of Salvation

God loves you—no matter who you are, no matter what your past. God loves you so much that He gave His one and only begotten Son for you. The Bible tells us that "...whoever believes in him shall not perish but have eternal life" (John 3:16 NIV). Jesus laid down His life and rose again so that we could spend eternity with Him in heaven and experience His absolute best on earth. If you would like to receive Jesus into your life, say the following prayer out loud and mean it from your heart.

Heavenly Father, I come to You admitting that I am a sinner. Right now, I choose to turn away from sin, and I ask You to cleanse me of all unrighteousness. I believe that Your Son, Jesus, died on the cross to take away my sins. I also believe that He rose again from the dead so that I might be forgiven of my sins and made righteous through faith in Him. I call upon the name of Jesus Christ to be the Savior and Lord of my life. Jesus, I choose to follow You and ask that You fill me with the power of the Holy Spirit. I declare that right now I am a child of God. I am free from sin and full of the righteousness of God. I am saved in Jesus' name. Amen.

If you prayed this prayer to receive Jesus Christ as your Savior for the first time, please contact us on the web at www.harrisonhouse.com to receive a free book.

Or you may write to us at
Harrison House
P.O. Box 35035
Tulsa, Oklahoma 74153

About the Author

Willie J. Hacking was in constant ministerial contact with Smith Wigglesworth for a period of over 25 years. He was a Pentecostal preacher who was born and raised in the United Kingdom. He spent many years of itinerant ministry at home and abroad in evangelism and Bible teaching. He and his wife, Florrie, were married for more than fifty-five years and had two children, four grandchildren and eight great-grandchildren. He passed away in October of 2001, at the age of ninety-nine.

Harrison House
Living Classics

Questions and Answers on Spiritual Gifts
By Howard Carter

Smith Wigglesworth—The Secret of His Power
By Albert Hibbert

Available from your local bookstore.

Harrison House
Tulsa, Ok 74153

The Harrison House Vision

Proclaiming the truth and the power

Of the Gospel of Jesus Christ

With excellence;

Challenging Christians to

Live victoriously,

Grow spiritually,

Know God intimately